eBay Made Easy

How to Quickly and Easily Make Thousands of Dollars Selling Everyday Items Online

By

Jay Johns

Disclaimer

This book is intended for educational purposes only and in no way guarantees any degree of success in online business. The author has made every attempt to verify that all information contained herein is correct to the best of his knowledge at the time of publication. However, this information is intended to be used as a reference by the reader. The author is in no way responsible or liable for any outcome that may result from a reader of this book entering into any form of online business activity. When selling on eBay as with any form of business you are entirely responsible for your level of success and for any outcomes, financial or otherwise, that result from your actions. Outcomes achieved vary from person to person based on level of skill, effort, and other circumstances. This book is purely a guide and does not guarantee any outcome; specifically, it does not guarantee any level of financial gain.

CONTENTS

Chapter 1 – The Foundation of Success 1

Chapter 2 – Learning the Ropes 7

Chapter 3 – What to Sell 13

Chapter 4 – Types of Listings 17

Chapter 5 – Types of Fees 25

Chapter 6 – Creating Your Listings..29

Chapter 7 – Getting Paid and Shipping..44

Chapter 8 – Your Money Plan 56

Final Thoughts 67

Chapter 1 – The Foundation of Success

How many times in the last month have you needed more money?

Just stop and think about that for a second. How many times have you been frustrated or stressed or just plain fed up with the pinching and squeezing it takes to juggle bills, the cost of gas and groceries, the kids' activities, debt that you just can't seem to make a dent in no matter how hard you try, and oh, yeah – things you want to do or stuff you'd like to buy just for enjoyment, like that new pair of shoes, tickets to that game or concert, or a vacation for your family?

It's exhausting, isn't it?

You're not asking to be a millionaire; you just don't want to be scraping and scrounging every time it's a few days before payday. Maybe you could even treat yourself to a little something every now and then.

Or maybe you're on the other side of the fence. Instead of trying to get ahead or live more comfortably, you got hit with some unexpected bad luck and just want to keep your head above water. Costly medical bills. An unforeseen job loss or injury that cut your work hours back. Increase in your rent or property taxes.

However you look at it, one thing is true – there are TONS of different circumstances where some extra cash would come in handy or even be a lifesaver for you and those who depend on you.

This book will teach you how to use eBay to make extra money by giving you a step-by-step proven formula for generating your first $1,000 in profit and then spring boarding yourself to a consistent side income without:

a) Getting another job where you work set hours for someone else who keeps most of what you make anyway
b) Being tied to what you're doing for any length of time or unable to take a break when you want
c) Having to design your own products or provide a service
d) Marketing, promoting, or doing any of the "salesy" stuff that you aren't good at

Probably the most beautiful thing about eBay is that it's massive enough to make you some serious money yet simple enough that it takes next to nothing to get started and become successful. It literally is whatever you want to make it.

I'm walking proof of the potential for eBay to change your life for the better. In November of 2012, my wife and I made a difficult decision to undergo fertility treatments after trying for years to have a child with no success. When the doctor told us the cost of the procedure, the medications, and all of the office visits, which weren't covered by insurance, my jaw didn't just drop, it plummeted. All in all it would come to the equivalent of nearly two years' worth of mortgage payments. Even with a nice little savings built up in our early years together, it wasn't exactly a sum we were just ready to drop in an instant. But we were determined to become parents; since we got married we knew we wanted to have children and after getting opinions from multiple doctors we knew that this was our only real hope of reaching that goal.

There was a payment plan available and some discount programs, but even with the help it was still a huge cost. We talked it over, but knew deep down we were going to go through with it no matter what. That's when my mind turned to eBay. I had bought and sold a few things on it before, maybe one or two a year, and didn't really know much about how it all worked let alone if it could be a legitimate source of extra money.

But we needed it, so I dug in and got started.

Without really knowing what I was doing I just sold and sold and sold. Anything I could get my hands on that I thought would turn a profit. And when the first sales started trickling in and then became more and more, and the cost of our treatments didn't seem so astronomically high any more, I knew I was on to something.

Fast forward to today, and not only are we proud parents, but I'm still selling on eBay. The extra money continues to be a huge help with the cost of raising a child, to do fun activities, and to enable my wife to stay at home.

As an eBay Power Seller who's sold over $26,000 (and still counting) in my free time, outside of my full-time day job and responsibilities as a father, husband, and homeowner, I've learned tons of tips and techniques over the years to identify items that will consistently sell for a profit and to get them listed, packed, and shipped quickly and efficiently. Instead of spending years learning by trial and error--like I did--you can grab up all of my knowledge in this series of books, for less than the cost of a sandwich for lunch.

I've turned it up a notch on eBay when I've had costly things coming up like family trips or holidays or when I got hit with some unexpected bills, and I've taken months almost completely off and still made a little bit of money while doing next to nothing from the work I already put in. I do it all totally on my own schedule, when I want to, and I don't have to answer to anyone telling me what to do or how to do it, though I've absolutely learned a ton by listening to people who've "been there," which is why I'm passing my experience on to you as a way to give back.

I'll be completely honest with you – this isn't one of those "Start an online business, quit your job, and do nothing but chill out on sandy beaches sipping cocktails while money comes pouring into your bank account as you sleep" books that you've probably already dabbled in online. This is a "your kid's summer camp costs $300 and you also have a wedding coming up this month and need to get a hotel room and a gift and a dress – so a few hundred bucks extra would really come in handy!" type of book. Plain and simple: I promise that if you put in the effort and follow the steps in this book and apply a little creativity, out of the box thinking and above all EFFORT, you can not only generate $1,000 of profit (if not more) in 60 days but also set yourself up to have a consistent stream of extra cash coming in each month.

Don't be the kind of person who hears about others achieving financial breathing room and even making "fun money" on eBay, but stays on the sidelines because it sounds like too much work, or something that's too complicated and intimidating. Be one of the people making positive changes for themselves and their families, the ones that others see and wonder how they do it when everyone else is stressing out about this bill and that cost going up. 90% of success is just getting started and showing up each day, so be the kind of person that doesn't wait!

The techniques you'll learn in this book have been proven to generate sales and profit on eBay across a number of different categories of items and for any level of sellers, including complete beginners who have never been on eBay before. All you have to do to learn them and start putting them to work for you is keep reading and then, most importantly, ACT! Each chapter and each book will give you more and more tools you can use to get yourself selling and making money and then boost your numbers so you're generating more profit in less time!

Chapter 2 – Learning the Ropes

Before you list your first item and make your first dollar (which won't take very long, by the way) you need to do some thinking. Let yourself know the reason why you're on eBay in the first place. Having a clear picture of why you're selling is the foundation that you can layer your knowledge on top of to become successful. Everyone has their own reason for selling on eBay, but at their core they're all the same: to make more money. Your individual variety of that could be because:

a) You're leaving a full-time job to start your own business and need a source of income to help you pay bills while you get your idea up and running

b) You lost your job unexpectedly, and need to make money to hold you and your family over

c) You want your family to be able to live on one income and afford to have a parent stay home instead of putting your child(ren) in daycare

d) You want to enjoy your retired years in comfort instead of living on a fixed income

e) You're a college student and need money for tuition, books, or living expenses

f) You want to be able to spend guilt free on things like going out, buying shoes, playing golf, or traveling

Whatever your reason(s) are, internalize them. Make sure you know exactly why you're getting into this, because when the going gets tough and you feel like throwing in the towel (making money on eBay is simple, but not automatic – there is definitely some hard work involved to get up and running) they're what will keep you driven to continue. People often start out really motivated on a project (think of everyone at the gym in January and February), but quickly fade if they don't have a solid goal to drive them. Being very clear with yourself about why you want to sell on eBay will push you to not only keep at it, but to learn more and get better so you can reap more rewards from your work.

This book is specifically designed to get you to your first $1,000 in profit from eBay. Why $1,000? For starters, that's a large enough amount of money to make a real difference in your life, whether it's in helping pay bills,   reduce debt, or to give you some "luxury" things you've always wanted but could never seem to afford. But more than that, $1,000 is significant because it proves that eBay is a viable way to generate extra cash.

You can make extra money mowing lawns or babysitting or detailing cars or doing a bunch of different things. But to make $1,000 without spending just as much time as you would working a full-time job you have to have a platform that's powerful enough to bring people who are willing and ready to spend money to you, where all you have to do is present them with something to spend their money on, instead of hunting down money-making opportunities.

Do you know how many doors you'd have to knock on or phone calls you'd have to make to get $1,000 worth of "extra work" in two months? If you can profit that much, you've proven that selling on eBay "works" as an effective way to make money that you can continue to grow (which we'll talk more about in Books 2 and 3, not to get ahead of myself!)

So now that we've established the groundwork to be successful, it's time for the X's and O's of selling – time to dig in and get some of the basic moves down so you can start getting paid! Exciting, isn't it? Well let's learn more…

The first step to selling on eBay is, simply enough, to create an account. To be specific, two accounts, one on eBay itself and another on PayPal. You may have heard of PayPal already. If not, it's an online payment processing platform that is the primary payment method used on eBay. You simply link your bank account to PayPal and then you're able to use it pretty much the same as a checking account. You can send money to another PayPal user the same way you'd give money to a friend to split the cost of lunch, pay for things you purchase, or receive money for things buyers purchase from you.

When someone purchases one of your items on eBay, PayPal will handle the transfer of funds from their account to yours.

There is a small transaction fee involved, as of the writing of this book it's 3% of the total sale plus 30 cents. Nobody likes fees, but honestly that's a very small price to pay for a pre-built platform that can handle all of the financial aspects of selling online, everything from refunds, withdrawals of your profits to your bank account, and all the rest in between.

Because you'll need to enter your PayPal account information when you sign up on eBay (so you can get paid!) we'll cover setting that up first. Both eBay and PayPal occasionally make updates to their appearance and so showing screenshots of how both interfaces look right now may be confusing down the road, so instead, I'm going to go over the steps to take to register for an account on each. While some names and things may change you can use these steps as a guide and if you have any confusion, both platforms offer very easy to follow instructions on how to register that will guide you through everything you need to do.

You start by going to www.paypal.com and clicking the Sign Up button in the upper right corner. You'll be offered two options for which type of account you want to create, Personal or Business. You'll select a Personal account and click Continue. If down the road you get to a point where you're consistently selling high amounts on eBay, meaning in the several thousands of dollars a month range, then you'll likely want to look into a Business account. For the beginner and even novice eBayer though a Personal account is just fine.

You'll then be prompted to enter your email address, which will be how PayPal identifies you and what you use to send and receive payments. While not necessary, it's a good idea to use the same email address that you plan to set up your eBay account just for the convenience of it. After this you'll be prompted to enter your full name, address, and phone number as well as to read and agree to PayPal's User Agreement.

Once you've done this, you now have a PayPal account. You can log in using your email address and the password you created earlier. The next steps to get your account fully functional are to link your bank account and then verify that it belongs to you, so PayPal knows that it's safe to withdraw from and deposit money to your account. PayPal offers great instructions on their website for how to complete this process, so just follow along step by step and you'll be ready to go in no time.

Alright, now that you have the financial part in order, it's time to create your actual eBay account. You'll go to ebay.com and follow the steps to register by clicking the "Sign Up" link. You'll list your basic information and also the email address that's linked to the PayPal account you just established. Once you do all of that you're pretty much ready to go. Similar to PayPal eBay's procedures can change slightly from time to time so ultimately you're just going to follow each of the steps on the screen. To put it bluntly, it's easy. Don't worry about anything complicated; just go step by step and you can have an account set up in minutes.

And just like that, you're up and running on eBay. Not difficult at all. Now that you have your account all set up and a way to get paid, it's time to dive into the selling – so buckle up, and let's do it!

Chapter 3 – What to Sell

This is where it gets good. After taking care of the stuff up front it's finally time to start selling! We're going to dive right in so you can get some money rolling in early and start to gain momentum. So much of being successful on eBay is weathering the early road, where things seem like they won't ever sell. I can't begin to tell you how many people I've known who have put a few things up for a 7-day auction, got no bids, and expertly declared that "that eBay stuff doesn't work." In other words, they didn't see big fat cash within days of starting a brand new endeavor, so they gave up.

But that's not going to be you, of course. Not only because you're wiser and much more motivated than that, but because you have three entire books worth of knowledge coming your way from a eBay Power Seller who has moved tens of thousands of dollars of so called "junk" for a profit over the years. And that's exactly where we'll start – junk.

The low, actually nonexistent (other than having access to the Internet) barrier to entry is one of the reasons eBay is such a great way to earn some cash quickly. I started selling regularly on eBay (I'd had an account for years but only sold a thing or two here and there for a long time) in late 2012 one Saturday afternoon by going through my closet and finding things I hadn't worn in a while or didn't fit me anymore. All in all, I had about six pieces of clothes. I took pictures of them with my phone, transferred them to my computer, and spent the next half hour or so creating the listings. By Wednesday of that week I had already made a sale.

That was all it took. Probably about an hour of work total and I not only made my first sale but also had a handful of other items that sold not too long after. I can't remember the exact figures but in just that batch of things alone I think I sold almost $150. Subtract out fees and shipping costs and I easily cleared over $100. That's right, a week ago this stuff was literally hanging in my closet, untouched for months. Now I had an extra $100 in my pocket. Examples like this just go to show how simple it really is to get started making money on eBay – how's that for motivation?

So, your first order of business is going to be an easy one that you'll probably end up enjoying. You're going to raid your house (or apartment, or dorm, or barracks room, or igloo – wherever you live) and drag out anything and everything you don't use or have a need for any more. How can you tell if you don't need it? Just be honest with yourself. We all have a little bit of hoarder mentality in us, keeping things because "we might use it/wear it/need it someday" but knowing deep down that we're just avoiding getting rid of it because psychologically we don't want to part with it.

So here's how we're going to start off on the right foot – by using your own psychology in your favor. One simple question to ask yourself as you rummage through your stuff and pull out anything that you don't use regularly: "Would I rather have this or money?" I'm not saying that every single thing you have and don't use is going to sell on eBay, nor am I saying that everything that does sell is going to bring in a big profit, but for it all to add up (and believe me, it does!) you have to first build the mindset that everything you own has a value, and if that value isn't being delivered in the use you get from it, then it's a monetary value that you're missing out on by letting it lay around untouched. Those old jeans or that sweater from a few seasons ago? Rather them or money? Espresso maker that you got as a Christmas gift from, yep, you can't even remember who – it or money? DVDs and video games you don't touch anymore because the entire entertainment universe has gone digital? Money would probably serve you better.

This is where you change your mindset and start thinking of what could be. If you sell only a few items you've already paid next month's cable bill, which means you have that much more money to put towards other things you need or want. So grab a big garbage bag (or several) and get at it – raid those closets, crawlspaces, attics, dressers, shelves, and cabinets and grab anything that you know deep down is just taking up space. Toss it all in the bag and think of the money you're going to turn it into. This is how I got started, how tons of other eBayers got started, and how you're going to get started too – and as you get into it you'll find that it feels refreshingly good.

Chapter 4 – Types of Listings

Now that you've gathered your set of "starter items" to sell, it's time to get them listed so people can actually see them and buy them. Listing on eBay is a very simple process, and once you get the hang of it you'll be able to knock out several items in just a few minutes each. For right now though we just want to focus on getting the first few items listed, so follow along as we're going to walk through every part of a listing so you can learn exactly what you need to do to get your stuff out there where millions of buyers are ready to fork over some cash for it.

I'll warn you up front this chapter is long because it covers a lot of information, but it's the critical "meat" of the knowledge you need to get started so pay attention. Break it into a few reading sessions if you need to so you can make sure you don't miss anything – it's that important.

Types of Listings – There are two ways you can sell your items (with a few variations on each), and depending on who you talk to, different opinions on which is better. I'll go over each here and give you my own experience on when and how to use each one by talking about how they've worked for me.

The first type of eBay listing is an auction, where, as the name implies, buyers bid on your item just as they would in a real-life auction. You set the starting price for bids and the duration is for a specific amount of time (you can choose, anywhere from three days up to ten, with the standard being seven.) At the end of the auction whoever is the highest bidder walks away the winner.

The other option is what eBay calls Buy it Now and is again, exactly what it says. Instead of bidding on an item against others, buyers can simply purchase it on the spot just as they would from any other store, either online or offline. You set a price and people buy; simple. This option is appealing to the type of people who either don't want to wait on an auction or don't want to risk coming up short against other bidders.

You can also combine the two, listing your item as an auction but also adding a Buy it Now option (this will cost you a little bit extra in listing fees, which we'll discuss in a bit) so that people can either take their chances bidding or just grab the item on the spot. You have to set your Buy it Now price at least 30% higher than the starting bid, so for example, you can't list an item as an auction with a $9.99 starting price and offer a $10.99 Buy it Now option.

eBay also offers sellers a Best Offer option that you can add to your Buy it Now listings for free. If you elect to use this, buyers can bargain with you, sending you their proposed price for you to accept, reject, or counter. For example, if you list something for sale at $50, a buyer may send you an offer of $25 and you can counter with $35. Buyers and sellers can go back and forth for three rounds of offer-counteroffer until the seller has to decide to either accept or reject whatever the offer at that point is. The following sections offer a little more detail on each type of listing as well as the pros and cons to choosing them.

Auctions – eBay originally started by offering only auction listings. Auctions are very good for getting views on your items, because people keep checking back to see what the current price on an item is and to decide whether they want to place a bid. As a rule of thumb, "regular" items, or things that aren't hard to get generally won't fetch as high of a selling price via auction simply because buyers aren't competing for them as much. On the other hand, "rare" or "vintage" items tend to do well as auctions because people are going to try to one up each other to win them since they're hard to come by. This isn't to say that you should never use auctions if you're only selling everyday items – they offer some advanced marketing benefits as they generate eyes on your items, which is a necessity.

Another advantage auctions offer is that they're more likely to sell than a Fixed Price Listing, which is also good at any time but especially when you're just getting started. Remember the eBay search algorithm that we talked about? It likes sellers who make sales. I personally use auctions to "get things going" with my listings if I'm in a slow spell or if I need to get up and running again after taking some time off. I know that if I make some sales with auctions, even though the profit might not be as high as a Fixed Price sale I'll get the spillover benefit of my items ranking higher in searches and generating additional sales as a result. Now again, I have to throw in the disclaimer that I didn't pick apart tons of eBay sales data to determine this with complete certainty, it's simply my observation from having sold tens of thousands of dollars – so in other words, real-world experience.

Auctions can range anywhere in duration from one day to ten days, with the "standard" being seven days. Your first 20 free listings each month are seven day auctions, and auction listings for durations other than seven days are charged an extra fee. In my experience seven days has been perfectly fine for duration. It gives plenty of time for enough people to see your item and bid on it and maybe even get into a bit of a bidding war which will drive up the price. Any shorter and you might not get to enough bidders' "price ceilings" or the maximum they're willing to spend, and any longer and your item loses some of its appeal by becoming stale. Of course there are opinions from other sellers on how and why you should use listing durations of other than seven days and they're probably entirely valid, but in my experience I've done perfectly fine with the standard (and for the first part of the month free) seven day listing.

Buy it Now – Buy it Now listings are the eBay equivalent of regular online shopping. After being an auction-only platform early in its existence, eBay wisely decided to capitalize on our growing impatience and added the Buy it Now feature. As I mentioned in the previous section, Buy it Now selling prices tend to run a little higher because sellers know that people really want an item, which of course makes it a little more valuable. The majority of my sales are Buy it Now because most of the items I sell aren't "competitive" items that would fit the auction model well, other than the traffic and initial sales generation that we talked about. With Buy it Now listings you have a bit more control as a seller because you can set an initial price but then adjust if you're not seeing any action, whereas if you set an opening bid on an Auction listing and a seller places one, that price now becomes the "benchmark" for further bidding up, even if it's lower than what you could get.

Buy it Now listings can range in duration anywhere from 3 days to 30 days, with a final option called "Good Till Cancelled" that is essentially an infinite listing that remains active until someone either buys the item or you end it. Buy it Now listings will incur a 30 cent insertion fee, so unlike free auctions you're on the hook for a small amount of cash. Good Till Cancelled listings automatically renew every 30 days and charge you the 30 cent rate each time. Once again, the question of listing fees comes into play, so I'll tackle it with my two cents (no pun intended) and experience.

Fees a necessary part of making money on eBay. Some folks will say they're only using free listings, to which I reply they're probably not selling much because they're only listing a handful of items a month. Why would you shy away from a 30 cent fee when in one sale you'll not only make that money back but also make enough profit to likely cover all of your listing fees for a given month? Also, remember the general tilt toward higher selling prices from Buy it Now versus Auctions? It's worth the few dimes to sell something as a Buy it Now when you're going to make more than that in profit over listing the item via the free route.

Auction with Buy it Now – This is a fairly common combination that has produced some good results for me because it plays on a buyer's psychology. They see an auction and read your description (which you wrote to focus on benefits, getting their "I want it" juices flowing – right?) and are ready to place a bid. Then the little Buy it Now button sucks them in further and they start thinking about the other folks out there that are also going to bid on it and whether someone is willing to go higher and outlast them. They really want it, so they give in and just hit Buy it Now and you've made a sale, quite possibly at a higher price than the auction would have climbed to.

Of course this doesn't happen every time but it does indeed happen, which is what makes this a useful tactic in your overall sales game plan. The downside is that you're charged a fee to add the Buy it Now option to your listings (10 cents as of the writing of this book), which means that if the item doesn't sell you're out that money. It's worth it for the potential upside in my opinion, but not all the time. I'd estimate that I add the Buy it Now option to about half of my Auction listings.

Buy it Now with Best Offer – I mentioned Best Offer earlier as an option that lets buyers and sellers negotiate a price, and I've used it several times to again "get things going" on my listings because it brings more buyer involvement. Instead of feeling as if the price for something is too high and moving on, buyers will stay engaged with your listing if they know there's a chance they can talk you down in price a bit. Obviously this means that if you plan to use the Best Offer option you have to set your starting price higher to account for some negotiating. Every so often you'll get a Buy it Now listing with best Offer that sells at the regular price, usually in cases where the person didn't mind the starting price and didn't want to go through the effort to negotiate or maybe for whatever reason just had to have the item as soon as possible. These cases are the exception though, so just be aware that if you go the Best Offer route you're going to end up selling your item for less than you priced it at to start.

eBay gives sellers the option to automate the Best Offer process, which comes in handy because it lets you take advantage of it without doing a lot of additional work. You can set lower and upper price limits so that any offer over a certain dollar amount is automatically accepted for a sale and any offer under a certain amount is automatically rejected.

Something key to remember here is that there are two different options if you don't like an offer – rejection or counter offering. Rejection is flat out telling the buyer "No" and not making them an offer in return, so in essence, something you might do if you feel there initial price was so low that there's not much chance the two of you could ever meet in the middle on something that works for both. Counter offering is the standard negotiating prices where you don't accept a buyer's offer but come back to them with something of your own. This part of the process can't be automated obviously, but if you do set lower and upper limits for your Best Offer listings then at least the only offers you'll have to manually handle are the ones that fall between those two prices.

Chapter 5 – Types of Fees

While eBay is about the most inexpensive way to get started making cash online especially if you don't have much startup money, it isn't free. You will pay certain fees to eBay when you list and sell items in exchange for being able to use their platform and be exposed to millions of buyers around the world. This chapter explains those fees so you understand exactly where the money you pay in fees is going and what you get for it.

Insertion Fees – These are costs you pay to eBay for the right to post your item for sale. Think of them as the virtual form of renting a booth at a flea market, except that they're much less expensive. You get a certain number of auction listings free to start each month and after that you're charged a fee for each additional listing. Fees vary depending on the type of listing you create and the category the item is in, generally anywhere from 10 to 30 cents. With auction listings you have the option to make your listing shorter (if you really want to sell an item soon) but the fees involved are somewhat higher. Also, if you list an item for auction but add a Buy it Now option, you'll be charged an additional fee.

When starting out on eBay people often get hung up against the idea of paying a fee to list items, which is absolutely the wrong way to think about things. Fees are only a fraction of a dollar regardless of which option(s) you choose for your listing, and considering that selling on eBay exposes you to millions of buyers literally all over the world, they're just the cost of doing business to get in the game. Think of it this way – if you tried to open your own online store, regardless of what you were selling, you'd basically be sitting there on your own with no buyers unless you paid an internet marketing consultant of firm a lot of money to get your store "out there" where people knew about it and came to your website. The internet is a big place, so trying to go it alone and hope people will find you and pay you for things just simply isn't a smart idea.

When you sell on eBay, the marketing part is already done for you because people come to eBay ready to buy things. You'd be foolish to not pay 30 cents to list something that you could sell for $30; basically one or two sales can pay for an entire month of listing fees. Also, eBay will run promotions from time to time (I haven't done any hard research on this but based on what I see offered to me I'm pretty sure the more active you are as a seller the more promotional offers you get) where you'll receive a large number of free listings, sometimes as many as 1,000, for a certain period of days. Take advantage of these when they come around and, combined with your free listings to start the month, you can cut your fees down as much as possible.

Final Value Fees – These are what people commonly refer to as "eBay taking a cut" when you sell something. Again, it's pretty simple – you pay a fee that's a certain percentage of the final selling price of your listing. The final price that your fee is calculated from includes shipping, which is a point of contention for lots of sellers who deal in large, heavy items that cost a lot to ship. This is understandable, since often times they're not making a profit on shipping but rather simply charging the buyer the same amount that the Postal Service charges them, yet are still stuck paying a fee on that cost. The reason eBay does this though is to prevent sellers from beating the system and getting around it by charging a nominal amount such as $1 for the item and having insanely high shipping charges that aren't subject to fees.

Like Insertion Fees, Final Value Fees also vary based on the category the listing is in. Fees for clothing, shoes, and accessories will be different than fees for antiques and collectables. Again, rather than list all of the current fee rates for each category, I'll just point out that eBay offers a very detailed explanation of its fees; you can refer them at any time to get the most current information. The same idea here is true – while some people will grumble about having to pay a 10% fee on a sale, smart people will realize that this is a drop in the bucket compared to what it would cost to make that same sale on your own without the use of eBay's platform. So in short, when it comes to fees, the mindset is simply "you gotta pay to play", because having access to the millions of worldwide eBay buyers is the key to being able to even make any sales at all.

That's a quick explanation of the basic fees associated with selling on eBay so you have enough knowledge to get started. There are certainly more complex fee scenarios if you get really advanced, but to just get up and running you only really need to understand how Insertion Fees and Final Value Fees work as those are the two you'll be dealing with most frequently.

Chapter 6 – Creating Your Listings

Listing items for sale on eBay is pretty simple and straightforward when you understand all of the information you need to enter. This chapter will walk you through each of them so you'll be buzzing through your listings in no time and getting things up for sale so buyers can start finding you.

To begin, you just click to the "Sell" link at the top of the page when you log in to your eBay account. You'll be given a prompt asking if you want to sell your item yourself or have eBay do it for you. eBay offers a service called eBay Valet where you can ship your items off and have an eBay representative take care of the listing and selling for you, for a fee that comes out of the sale profit. I've never used this service for two reasons – first, most of the items that I sell don't meet the qualifications for being able to use it, but more importantly because I don't want to part with a portion of my profits. Granted, if you were selling a lot of high value items a service like this would absolutely be a worthwhile investment, assuming you had more inventory to sell than you had time to work on it, but for most beginner eBayers this simply won't be the case. I always keep it in the back of my mind, but just haven't got to a point where I think it would be worth the investment or giving up control of the selling process.

That said, the rest of this book is going to focus on how to list items for sale yourself. We'll do it by first walking through each of the pieces of a listing so you understand what information you need to provide, why it's important, and how to best use it in your favor to make a sale. The final section will then lay out a step-by-step plan for you so all you have to do is tailor it to your specific situation and follow the steps to your first $1,000!

Category – The first piece of information you need to determine when you create a new eBay listing is the category the item is in. eBay offers hundreds of different categories very similar to how regular store websites are divided. Categories range from Antiques and Collectibles, Clothing, Electronics, and everything in between. When you enter the title of what you're selling (more on how to do that the best possible way in a minute), eBay will automatically provide a few suggestions of categories that your item likely falls into based on the wording of the title. Nine times out of ten one of those is going to be the best one, so all that you have to do it pick it from the list provided by clicking on it, and you're all set. If for some reason you think your item should be listed in a different category though, you can just browse all of the available categories and find the one that you prefer. They're organized in a parent-child format, with each larger category breaking down into smaller sub-categories so you can logically follow them.

Don't put a ton of thought into picking which category you'll list your item in. Simply pick the one that's the most applicable, and move on. The reason for this is that most eBay buyers search for items by name rather than browsing categories, so having a relevant and descriptive title is going to benefit you far more than trying to strategically place your item in a category where you think it will get more views (hint: if it doesn't belong there it can get all the views under the sun, but it's not going to make any sales because buyers are looking for things that actually are part of that category.)

One final word on category, which is actually more of an overarching principle for selling. Some sellers will also try to outsmart eBay by placing their item in the category that has the lowest final value fees, again whether it belongs there or not. Don't do it. It's just not good practice, and while you may get away with this a few times eBay isn't some fly-by-night operation that isn't smart on all the ways people try to gain an advantage. Your account can be suspended for violating selling policies, and trying to cheat the system like this or in any other form will eventually catch up with you. You don't need any clever tricks to sell and make money on eBay; just do what makes sense and leave it at that.

Title – Your listing title is critical. It's not only the first thing prospective buyers will see, which is the obvious reason for its importance, but in the "behind the scenes" part of eBay that determines which listings out of the millions posted come up when a buyer enters a specific search, the words in the title play a large part in determining if that listing will be shown and also how high up the list it appears. Think of searching the internet for anything – when was the last time you went beyond the first page or two (maybe three if you're really looking hard) of results to find what you want? You probably stick to the highest results, and eBay buyers are no different. A small portion will scroll through hundreds of listings but most will look at the top few to find what they want and ignore the rest.

Your title should contain keywords that people searching for an item are likely to enter. Things like the brand of an item, style, color, material, and design are all important details that you want to have in your title so buyers can find your listing. If your item is a collectible or antique, you'll want to include the time period or maybe even the exact year it's from, such as a 1920's vintage ceramic vase. I just made that up since I know nothing about vases, but just to illustrate the point. When creating your title just put yourself in a buyer's shoes – ask "If I were searching for this, would this title let me know this item is what I'm looking for?"

Too often you'll see sellers make the mistake of being too vague, thinking that because clearly they know what their item is that buyers will too. Making a listing title that reads "Polo Ralph Lauren Short Sleeve Shirt" might seem fine if you're selling one from your closet that you're familiar with, but someone searching is likely going to want one for a specific gender and size at a minimum, and likely a certain style such as a polo shirt or a t-shirt and maybe even a certain color as well. If you were to go with the vague title we mentioned earlier, you'd most definitely lose out to someone who is selling the exact same item as you but makes their title read "Polo Ralph Lauren Men's Short Sleeve Polo Shirt Medium Green." You get over 80 characters for your title, so make sure you use them to your advantage by being as descriptive as possible.

One note though – DON'T do what is known as "keyword stuffing" by throwing in words that don't really pertain to your item just to help it get noticed in searches. An example of this would be including the name of a specific famous golf player in the title of a listing for a souvenir hat from a tournament. Unless the player autographed the hat or was otherwise directly associated with it somehow, using their name in the title in hopes of picking up views of your listing just because they're likely searched a lot in other contexts (for example, photos and memorabilia) is a violation of eBay policy. Over the years eBay's computer algorithm for reviewing listings has become a lot more sophisticated and can detect cases where sellers are just jamming unnecessary words in their title trying to trick the search process. This can result in a warning or even suspension of your selling account, so steer clear of it. Even if you get away with it from the computer review perspective, you'll only hurt yourself by disappointing buyers who go to your listing because it contains certain words only to find out your item isn't really what you're advertising it as. This is a good way to get buyers to mark you as a seller to avoid, so keep your title words absolutely relevant to the item you're selling.

Subtitle – This is one of several paid "listing upgrades" that eBay offers which are supposed to give you increased visibility in search results. In addition to your standard title, for a small fee (50 cents as of the writing of this book) you get another line of text to list even more information and details about your item. I guess it's useful to some people because eBay keeps offering it, which means people keep buying it, but I can say I have never, not one single time, used this or any other paid listing upgrades and I've done just fine selling – so I don't think it's necessary, especially not for a part-time seller.

Seller Notes – Depending on which category you're listing in, you may be offered the option to enter Seller Notes. This is a free text entry where you type anything the buyer may need to know about the item, such as its condition or any imperfections or errors it has. An example of one category where Seller Notes are included in listings is Used Clothing. If you were selling a pre-owned shirt that had a small snag or stain, you'd just include this in the seller notes so buyers are aware of it. One tip I've found to work well for this is to simply enter 'See Description for full details' and then describe your item in depth in the Description section of the listing, which we'll cover in a bit. This saves you from writing the same things out twice but also helps prevent buyers from leaving your item right away from the "sticker shock" of seeing that an item may have some flaws to it when they could be very minor and not impact its value much.

Photos – Photos, like your title, can really make or break your listing. Imagine two sellers each listing the exact same item. The first seller has one photo in her listing, and it's relatively poor quality – blurry, not very good lighting, and clutter of her kitchen table in the background. The other seller has eight photos; each one is clear and taken against a white background so you can see the details of the item close up as if it were sitting right in front of you without anything else to distract you. Which listing are you more likely to spend time reviewing and consider buying? It's simple – photos are very important if you want to make lots of sales on eBay!

The good news is that you don't have to be a professional photographer or have any fancy equipment to take great photos. I use the camera on my phone and a white plastic shower curtain that I bought on eBay (of course) for four bucks and my photos turn out great each time. You're allowed to add up to 12 photos for free to each eBay listing; more than that will incur an additional fee. I've never added more than 12 photos to a listing and I also have never used any of the photo-related listing upgrades that eBay offers such as Gallery Plus, which display your photos larger in search results. They may be useful but as with other paid listing upgrades, I've been able to make sales just fine without them.

This is good news for you, because all you have to do is focus on those simple basic aspects of photography and you'll do fine. Make sure your photos are clear and in focus -- blurry doesn't help the buyer see the detail of your item. Make sure you have a clean background. White tends to work well for a number of different items, but whatever you choose just avoid clutter in the background. Some people take photos on their kitchen counter or living room floor, which can be fine as long as the item is clearly shown, but a plain white background gives an extra look of quality and professionalism that can attract more buyers. Use proper lighting. If you use a phone camera, since in today's age that's the most readily accessible camera to nearly all of us, turn on the flash as necessary to provide adequate lighting. It also helps a ton to take your photos in a room with good overhead light. I do most of my photography in my garage, where the lights are high up on the ceiling directly above where I place my items. To sum it up, photography can most definitely make you sales that others miss out on, so take the time to do a good job at it.

Item Specifics – The Item Specifics section is the first place where you really give potential buyers the low down on what you're selling. The information included in this section is tailored to the category – for example, in the Clothing and

Accessories category some of the Item Specifics fields include Size, Color, Style, and Sleeve Length. In the Electronics category Item Specifics deal with the technical aspects of the item such as memory space for a computer hard drive or voltage for a battery. You get the drift; Item Specifics are, as their name states, specific details about the item that help buyers determine if it's exactly what they're looking for. These pieces of information are very useful for distinguishing similar variations of an item from each other; different lines of the same overarching product like a shirt or a cell phone, for instance.

Some of the Item Specifics will be required for the listing while others will be optional. Required Item Specifics are essential to helping inform buyers about the item while the others are more "nice to have" details that are useful but not critical. eBay has a pre-populated menu of options for each of the Item Specifics fields so you can just select the correct one for your item from the drop down menu. There is also an "Enter Your Own' option for you to type in information if your item isn't included in one of the provided selections, for example, a brand of clothing that might not be listed.

Fill in as many of the Item Specifics fields as you possible can. eBay's search algorithm looks closely at the information in the Item Specifics section of the listing when determining which items to show to buyers, so leaving fields blank can cause you to miss out on this opportunity. Aside from that, in cases where potential buyers do stumble upon your item just by chance even if it isn't ranking high in search results, they'll be less likely to purchase it because of the lack of detail. Even if you type all of the relevant information about your item into the Description section, don't just assume that buyers will actually read it. I've encountered many instances where I had information in the Description section but still received messages from buyers asking questions about an item that clearly showed they didn't read it, so fill in everything you can for the Item Specifics.

Description – The Description section of a listing is where you can type in anything you want to tell buyers about your item. This includes all of the details we talked about in the Item Specifics section and also other important things that may not fit into one-word entries from a drop down menu. The Description section can often be what pushes an on-the-fence buyer over to your side and gets them to click the "Buy it Now" or "Place Bid" button. If you describe your item in a clear, concise way and really help buyers understand exactly what you're offering and the condition it's in they'll be much more likely to purchase from you than from someone who leaves the Description section blank or just enters a sentence or two.

I'm going to walk you through my proven process for writing item descriptions that capture people's attention and make them more inclined to buy your item so that you don't have to scratch your head and struggle to figure out what to write each time. Of course you'll need to modify this slightly for different categories of items, but the basic outline will work for anything you sell, so here it is:

a) Write exactly what the item is. This seems overly simple, but is something so many people overlook. They think because they named the item in their Title they don't need to do it again in the Description. If you're selling a Polo Ralph Lauren Blue Men's Short Sleeve Polo Shirt Size large, then write that.

b) Put brand names, specific identifying terms, or other "keywords" in all caps the first time you use them. This is something that, while I don't have any hard data on, has appeared to give me a small boost in views and sales since I've started doing it. Perhaps eBay's algorithm has a condition that recognizes words in all caps more prominently or maybe it's just that caps get more attention from the reader which causes them to continue reading further and get more interested as they go, but whatever the reason this has seemed to help me out so I'd recommend it. It's not going to make a huge difference by a longshot, but every little bit helps when it comes to getting eyes on your items, because eyes are potential dollars being spent. One important note – notice that I said do this the FIRST time. If you do it all the time you'll get the opposite effect; annoyed readers for sure and possibly (again, I don't have hard data but just making an educated guess) unhappy eBay computers. So do it once for the effect and then go back to normal text.

c) List all details of the item. This includes measurements, sizes, years, makes, models, and anything else that would help inform a person. Brevity is the key here, without leaving anything out of course. You don't have to write in sentences and paragraphs, in fact, you're more likely to get someone's attention if you just list things in "bullet point" format. When you write in paragraphs words tend to get lost among each other in cases where someone is reading quickly, like a product description. As you write out your details, try to think of any questions you'd ask someone if you were buying the item. If you'd ask it, chances are someone who will view your listing would too, so include the answer in your details.

d) Make sure you include details about the condition of the item. If it's like new then say so. If it has some small scratches, stains, stains, or other flaws then state those. The purpose of doing all of this is so you're "covered" in the event a buyer gets an item and tries to claim you didn't disclose the condition and asks for a refund because of it. Being able to fall back on having these types of facts in your Description can definitely be to your advantage should you end up in a dispute (which in my experience aren't very common, but do happen) so anything about your item that qualifies as "not brand new" should be spelled out clearly so there's no confusion for the buyer.

e) Be polite. This may seem trivial but you'll find as you get more involved with eBay that for whatever reason lots of sellers like to be mean in their descriptions by writing all of the things they won't do such as ship faster or accept different types of payment than PayPal or bargain on prices. It's fine if you have a set of standards you want to sell by, but why risk coming off as mean and not a pleasure to do business with to a random person the first time they come into contact with your listings? I'm glad when sellers in the same categories that I work in do this because I know it just means more buyers will be put off by their listings and come looking elsewhere – including mine. Give off a happy and friendly tone in your Description. Show that you're probably someone who will be easy to do business with and that the buyer can trust. As you get more established you can definitely include a sentence (but not more, because you need to stay focused on the actual item) that makes note of your strong reputation and eBay Feedback score. In short, just project the kind of tone you'd want to read if you were buying an item. It will go a long way toward making people more likely to spend their money with you.

f) Talk about benefits. This is an area where so many eBay sellers miss out on an opportunity to really convert those "on the fence" buyers by not playing to their psychological need to realize the benefits of what you're selling them. Yes, your Description has to first be based on features of your item – the things we talked about like size, color, voltage, year, and so forth. But those are just details and aren't always going to be enough to convince a person to open up their PayPal account.

When you focus on benefits, you get the buyer thinking about what purchasing your item will do for them. If it's a piece of clothing, you can talk about how it will make them look cool in front of their friends. If it's an electronic device, you can talk about the convenience it will bring them or the problem it will solve, such as not having to deal with a drained phone battery at 4 PM if you're selling one of those extra-long battery life extenders. The classic example of benefits that I use is a handyman service. It's one thing to sell by saying you can do a bunch of different jobs around the house. However, it's an entirely different level of selling, one that's much more effective, to say that you can get a guy's wife off of his case about lingering home repairs by doing them for him in a fraction of the time and with no hassle. In a situation like that, where you play to a person's true desires (for our example husband, the desire to not have his loving wife bug him about home repairs so he can go play golf or watch football on the weekends) price almost becomes trivial as you're eliminating something that hits the "nerve" of a person. So think about what having your item can do for a person and write a few lines directly addressing that. Will it make things easier for them? Will it bring them social status? Will it be a "notch in their belt" so to speak if they're a collector? Hit the nerve, and you'll see people pulling out their cash much more freely.

Chapter 7 – Getting Paid and Shipping

For most Buy it Now listings your buyer will pay immediately or fairly soon after purchasing simply because eBay displays a prompt to initiate payment right after a person clicks the Buy button. There are some cases where buyers won't be so timely, which we'll discuss in a bit, but for the most part you'll get paid as soon as you make a sale. For Auction listings there can be a little bit of a delay because a buyer's winning bid may have been set by "auto bid" where they enter the maximum price they're willing to pay and just leave it alone, letting eBay automatically place bids for them up to the dollar amount they indicate. If this is the case, lots of buyers won't actually be at their computer entering a bid when the auction ends, so there can be a bit of a delay between the sale and payment, especially if your auction ends during standard working hours or at night; basically times when most people won't be on eBay.

There is an option in eBay where sellers can require immediate payment for Buy it Now listings, or Auctions with a Buy it Now option. This can come in useful to deter buyers who aren't serious about how they conduct themselves on eBay and can prevent you from having to wait for payments when you sell items. I've rarely used it though; to be honest in my years of experience I've found that most eBay buyers are actually honest, on the level, and will pay for things they purchase in a timely manner. Of course I run into the occasional bad apple, just as you will in any endeavor, but I'd estimate that fewer than 2% of my eBay transactions involve any kind of payment delay issues. So this is an option to consider but not something I'd call a necessity.

You may ask if there's any reason why you shouldn't use immediate payment if it's available so you know you'll get paid right away – which is a valid question. The reason is because requiring on the spot payment will definitely deter a certain segment of buyers. Just like in other payment scenarios, people are juggling bills and costs for this and that and everything else, so they may really want an item you're selling and be willing to pay for it but just not have the money available until their next payday. If you require immediate payment then you've excluded a willing buyer, whereas if you'd be open to waiting a few days to get paid you'd have made a sale. I've had buyers literally message me after purchasing items saying they'll pay as soon as they get their next paycheck at the end of the week and as I said earlier, the vast majority follow through.

Shipping, Handling, and Returns – After your payment terms the next part of your listing to complete is the Shipping and Handling details, which clearly spell out to buyers when and how you'll deliver their item to them once they purchase it. In this section we'll go through the available options and talk about some helpful tips so you can save money on your shipping costs while still delivering great service to your buyers.

Handling – Handling time is simply the time from when the buyer purchases and pays for an item until you actually deposit it in a mail drop of some sort for it to be shipped to them. This accounts for the time you'll need to package the item, purchase and print your postage, and deliver it for shipment. You'll indicate the number of days for handling time as part of your listing. eBay measures handling time in business days, so weekends and federal holidays don't count. I've read many places that listings with quicker handling time, specifically one business day handling, will get better visibility in search results. In my own experience, I have found this to be true.

The only thing to keep in mind with handling is that one of the seller rating metrics that eBay tracks and uses to determine your seller status is the number of items that you didn't upload shipping information for within the specified handling time. This gives the buyer a bad experience from thinking they'll be getting their item sooner than they do, so before you just choose one day handling for everything you sell, consider how long it will realistically take you to have it packaged and out the door. If it's a shirt hanging in your closet, it'd be no trouble to place it in a small shipping bag and leave it in the mailbox the next day. However, if you're dealing with a large kitchen appliance or a fragile antique piece of china that you'll need to carefully pack, doing this in one day after the sale might not be realistic.

In the end, if you can commit to one day handling it's in your best interest to do so, but if you're not able to meet this deadline choose something more reasonable based on your schedule rather than delivering your item late.

Shipping – eBay has built in options to offer shipping service from the U.S. Postal Service, UPS, and FedEx, though the vast majority of eBay packages are shipped via the Postal Service. Again throwing in my personal experience, I've never shipped via any other method than USPS and nearly every one of my thousands of transactions has gone very smoothly. The eBay shipping interface is simple and easy, providing sellers the ability to pay for and print their shipping labels directly from their eBay account just by entering the weight and dimensions, if applicable, of their item. When you do, Pay Pal will automatically deduct the cost of postage from your balance. A big advantage of this, aside from the convenience of having it in one interface, is that you get the online rates offered by the USPS which are anywhere from 5-20% lower than regular in-office rates. In addition, eBay sellers get free tracking on their shipments through the USPS, so you can always see where your item is and when it's delivered to the buyer. The two methods of USPS shipping are First Class and Priority, and we'll go over when each is used and things to be aware of next.

First Class Mail – Items weighing 16 ounces or less can be shipped via First Class U.S. Mail. The one exception to this is items that have dimensions which fall outside of the USPS guidelines for First Class postage. As of the writing of this book I believe those are 12 inches on any one side, though to be sure just check the most current requirement when you sell something. eBay asks if your item exceeds these dimensions when you choose your shipping method so you won't go unaware of it by mistake. You can package a First Class item in any sort of envelope or, something popular with a lot of eBay sellers depending on the type of items they sell, a 10 inch by 13 inch poly mailer bag – one of those plastic shipping bags that has the self-sealing strip on the end. First Class items can be placed in a regular mailbox, so the one at the end of your driveway, in the lobby of your apartment building, or the big blue ones on any street corner all work fine, just drop it in and that's it.

Priority Mail – Anything weighing more than 16 ounces has to be sent via Priority Mail, which costs more but is also delivered faster. When you purchase Priority postage you'll again be asked to enter your item's weight and whether it is over a certain set of dimensions in size. These two factors plus the zip code you're shipping to are all used to determine the total postage cost. Priority postage rates are tiered on the pound, so you'll pay for up to the next highest full pound of freight.

USPS also offers Flat Rate Priority shipping boxes in an assortment of sizes ranging from envelopes to small, medium, and large boxes. With these, anything up to a certain weight threshold, 70 pounds for a number of the boxes, can ship for one set rate. The nice advantage of this is that the boxes themselves are free from the Postal Service. You can order them online and have them delivered right to your door, so you don't have to spend time searching for shipping boxes or clutter a closet or room in your house saving old boxes. The downside, in some cases, is that you can overpay depending on where your item's weight falls. For example, you could have an item that fits into a medium Flat Rate box, which costs (as of the writing of this book) around $11, but might only cost $9 if you packed it yourself. This is just the way the math shakes out; the USPS offers a price that obviously will cover their costs for all shipments, so sometimes you may end up on the wrong side of that equation and would be better served cost-wise to pack an item yourself.

Probably the biggest advantage of Priority Mail is that the USPS provides free pickup service for it. You can go to the USPS website and schedule pickup from your home by just listing the number of items you have and approximate weight of each, then just leave them at the place you indicate for the mail carrier to pick up. This is one of the most unknown features of USPS shipping; I can't begin to count how many eBay sellers I know that still drive their packages to the Post Office every time they sell something. The tools offered by USPS really are great, so you should definitely put them to use.

Free Shipping vs. Calculated – In addition to determining which shipping service you'll use to send your items you also have to list the cost of shipping to buyers, just the same as any retail website does. There are a few different ways to approach this. The first, and my personal recommendation, is to offer free shipping. Buyers love free shipping just because it pulls one of those psychological levers to purchase (as does anything free) that we talked about a little bit before. There's also talk, and I'll support it with my own experience, that listings with free shipping get a boost in search standings. I ran a little experiment on this for about a month one time and my listings with free shipping significantly outsold those for the same types of items that I listed a shipping cost for, even when it was very reasonable.

When you offer free shipping you need to know with near certainty what it will cost you to ship your item so you don't wind up losing money in the process. Fortunately the USPS website offers a rate calculator where you just enter the weight of your item and the zip codes you're shipping to and from and it will give you the cost of various different postage options. Obviously you won't know where your buyer is located until after your item sells, so when determining how much to add to the price to make sure you completely cover shipping, a trick I use is to type in the zip code 90210. The reason for this is because I live on the east coast, and it's the only west zip code I know (from the show of course) so it gives me an estimate of what it will cost me if the buyer ends up being as far away in the U.S. as possible (we'll get into international shipping in just a bit.) I know that if my cost to ship all the way to California is going to be $7 then I'll be covered no matter where the buyer ends up being from if I use that as my amount to add to the item price.

The second shipping option is to specify a flat cost on top of the item price that is the same for all buyers regardless of their location. Some sellers do this and purposely make the cost higher than what they know it will be to ship the item so they make some money on it. This is perfectly fine, as the charge is by definition "Shipping and Handling" so the extra money is the handling portion that covers their packing materials, time, and other costs involved in getting the item out to the buyer. Finally, you can also offer what is called "calculated Shipping" which means that eBay will automatically determine the shipping cost after an item sells based on the type of service you select and the buyer's zip code. This method gives the true shipping cost, so there is no way to pad it to account for materials or time unless you enter the item's weight as being higher than it is. Of the two non-free shipping options this one usually appeals to more buyers because they're inclined to feel that a flat shipping charge is too high for them, knowing that it has to be set to account for all possible item destinations.

All of those considerations in mind, I again recommend going with free shipping. Aside from the search standing benefit, free shipping also removes any opportunity for buyers to rate you low on shipping costs because they feel they are too expensive (shipping speed and cost are two of the factors buyers leave feedback on when they rate the sellers they purchase from.) Free shipping eliminates the perception to buyers that you're overcharging for shipping and gives them an "out the door" total cost right up front when they look at your listing, which most will appreciate.

International Shipping – One of the biggest areas of mystery to eBay sellers, not just beginners but even those who have been selling for a while, is international shipping. A lot of sellers are weary of shipping to international buyers or don't know how to do it and as a result miss out on a lot of sales by excluding willing buyers. eBay actually makes selling and shipping to international buyers very easy by converting currency so you only need to list your item in U.S. dollars and the buyer will see and pay the corresponding price in their own currency. eBay will also add in any applicable tariffs or import fees so you don't have to worry about those either; buyers automatically see their final price with all costs included.

There are two options when shipping internationally. One is to use eBay's Global Shipping Program, which I've always thought is a great resource. When you ship an item via the GSP, you simply ship your sold item to a waypoint in the U.S., the exact same way as you would any domestic shipment. From there eBay handles the rest of the work, shipping the item on to its final destination. You are paid for the sale as you would be on a normal domestic sale, and eBay adds the additional shipping cost on to the buyer's purchase price to cover the international postage from the U.S. facility to their international address, with that part all being transparent to you. There are a series of eligibility criteria to use the GSP that include your own seller rating as well as the destination country, item category, and package weight and dimensions. If your listing meets all of the criteria though I strongly recommend using this option as it opens you up to many more buyers without requiring any additional effort on your part than would be necessary to complete a sale to a buyer in the U.S.

Your other international shipping option is the standard way – using an international service from the USPS or another carrier. If you do this, you will indicate when entering your listing which countries you'll ship to. You'll also select an international service from the menu provided by eBay and list a cost for the shipment so that if an international buyer purchases your item eBay can apply the extra postage cost to the sale. International shipments require a customs form so you'll have to complete this extra step that is handled by eBay when you use the GSP. You can schedule pickup of International shipments the same way that you can for domestic Priority ones, but if your customs form is incomplete or not filled out correctly your item will be left at the pickup point and you'll have to take it to a post office to send it. This can get to be a time consuming process even though the steps are fairly simple so my advice is to use the GSP whenever possible to eliminate as much of the extra work as you can.

Affixing Labels – I've used two methods for affixing labels to shipments which aren't much different from each other, though both have some pros and cons. The most basic method is to just print your labels on regular white printer paper, cut them out, and tape them to your package using clear tape. This works great, though when you start to sell more items, you'll find that it can be a time-consuming process to cut and tape several labels each day. Once I started seeing consistent heavy sales I started using shipping label stickers similar to what regular retailers use to ship items. You can buy them at most office supply stores or, even easier, on eBay. In fact, I've only ever purchased them on eBay and it's not hard to find a good price of less than ten cents per sheet. They come two half-sheet labels to a standard letter size page, and you just feed the sheets through your printer, peel your labels off, and stick them to your package.

The only downside is that when you have an odd number of shipments for a given print run you're left with a sheet that has one label sticker, so you wind up trying to combine all of your extras to keep things to two stickers per page. Not a huge deal, but a pain nonetheless. These labels of course cost more than regular printer paper, but I've never done any hard math on label cost versus the cost of tape to affix paper labels. My guess is they'd come out about the same, so given that my vote is for the label stickers because of the ease and time savings they offer.

Returns – The final piece to any eBay listing is the return policy. This is where you let your buyer know whether you'll accept returns if they get the item and decide they don't want it and if so, how long the return period is. You also indicate who pays for return shipping to get the item back to you (I've never known a seller who didn't require buyers to pay return shipping), and if you charge what is called a restocking fee for returns. Sellers often use the restocking fee as a way to recoup their shipping cost on a returned item. Again, eBay offers incentives in the form of better search result standing for listings that include a return policy.

You have a few options to choose from for the duration of your return period; 14 days is the minimum, and 30 and 60 days are the other options. You also indicate whether you will issue a refund for returned items, provide a replacement, or allow the buyer to exchange for another item. I always make my return period 30 days; this gives buyers more than enough time to decide that they don't want or need an item. I require buyers to pay return shipping and I issue cash refunds for returned items, provided the item is in the same condition that it was in when I sent it. I generally don't get many return requests; the best way to avoid them is to follow all of the guidelines we discussed earlier for writing clear item descriptions and to fill in all of the item specifics so that they buyer knows exactly what to expect.

Chapter 8 – Your Money Plan

Congratulations! By reading up to this point you now know what it took me close to five years to learn about eBay. Not bad for a buck and an hour or so of your time, huh? Want to know what's even better? There's still more to go – and since what you've learned up to this point is the foundation, the rest of this book and the others in this series are all about making money! So here we go – your proven blueprint to making your first $1,000 on eBay.

The first step is to fully know what all you have to sell, because it will determine how much money you can potentially make. This habit, knowing the total potential value of your inventory, is a good one to get into early on because it helps you know when you need to go hunting more items. Too often I see new sellers wanting to make a specific amount of money, say $300, $500 or more, who don't have the necessary inventory to support those goals. Knowing at all times the potential profit of your items will keep you focused on the other things you need to do to reach your goals.

Make a List – Remember all of the items you found in your home earlier when we talked about things you don't need or use anymore? Write all of them down on a list. A spreadsheet on your computer will work best for this because we're going to be doing some math, but if you want to just use a sheet of paper and do the math by hand that's fine also. This list is going to be the basis of your potential profit calculation, so we're going to make sure that in order to make $1,000 we start out with at least that much in potential profit between all of the items we have to sell.

Research Sale Prices – eBay has an option that lets you search what price items have sold for, which is exactly the information you need to begin turning your list into a profit blueprint. To do this, you simple type the item name (using the same words that you'd use for the title when you create your listing) in the search box and then click the 'Advanced' button. On the next screen, check the box next to 'Sold Items' so you see only results for items that have sold. On this page there are other criteria available like 'Free Shipping' and 'Condition' so check all that apply to your exact item so you're comparing apples to apples. For example, if you're offering free shipping but comparing your prices against listings where the buyer pays shipping you're already out of the ballpark on price so make sure you pay attention to this. When you click 'Search' after applying all of the relevant filters you'll get a list of items exactly like yours that have sold and what their final prices were. Using the 'Sort' option you can look at the most recent results by picking 'End Date: Recent First' or you can check them out by price by changing this option to see what the high and low end is.

When you scan the listings, you'll get a general feel for what the going rate is for an item. There are always going to be outliers on both the high and low sides, situations where people priced their item way too low and others where either by luck or someone really wanting something badly it went for much more than it normally would. In general though you'll see prices start to group together around an average rate, which I've found is usually a good indicator of what you can reasonably expect to fetch when selling one of the same. Make sure to also view all of the sold prices by End Date also though; in rare occasions things may happen that could dramatically change the market value of an item from what it was a few weeks earlier. An example of this would be a sports player being traded to a different team, making his jersey from the old team no longer as sought after as it was when he played for them and thus driving down the price.

The Math That Adds Up to $1,000 – You're now going to use this information to project what each item on your list could sell for. The reason we're going to go with an in the middle value for selling price is to create a realistic projection. If an item has lots of sales around the $10 price point but two of them sold for $30, it wouldn't be reasonable to expect to get $30 for it and you'd be giving yourself unattainable projections. Go down your list of items and add the price that, based on your research, you believe each of your items will sell for.

Once you've completed this step you're going to add up all of the potential sale prices. This is your first check to make sure you're putting yourself on the right track to make $1,000. If your total adds up to less than $1,000 or barely over it, you need to adjust your course here because you don't yet have enough items to support your profit goal. This isn't cause for alarm; in fact it's pretty common when you're just starting out and is a good thing because it gets you focused on building inventory and listings up front.

So just how many items do you need? Well, let's do some backwards math to find out. A good general rule of thumb to determine the value of total sales after eBay and PayPal fees are taken out is around 85% - so if you want to make $1,000 you'd need to sell $1,000 / .85 or $1,176. Note that this is based off of no acquisition cost for your items, meaning you didn't pay anything to get them, you just already had them. Since this is the case for your early sales of items you have laying around the house, we don't have to subtract out any other costs.

Now that you know you have to sell around $1,176 worth of items, you can use your list to figure out, based on the average selling price of the things you have, about how many sales you'll need to make. Of course your sale prices are probably going to be all over the board since you're selecting anything and everything, but this is totally fine. As you become a more advanced seller you'll start to work primarily in certain niches, or categories of items, and you'll have a more consistent average selling price. For now, just determine the average of what you have. If there are any extreme outliers among your items that have a much higher or lower selling price than the others, exclude them from your calculation so it's more realistic. I looked back at my early selling days and found that my average sale prices were in the $10-13 per item range since I was selling mostly clothes and household goods, so a figure around here will probably be what you come up with also. If you get an average higher than this and you have some items that do in fact fetch higher prices on eBay then great – you're off to an even better start!

Divide the $1,176 total number by this average sale price figure and you'll get the approximate number of sales you'll need to make. You're probably going to end up somewhere between 90 and 120 sales necessary to reach that figure. Again, seeing numbers like that often causes beginners to panic because when in your mind you can count on one hand the few old shirts and other stuff you think you can sell sales count numbers around 100 seem like complete pipe dreams. Again, all totally normal. Once you spend some time researching sold items listings on eBay you'll be surprised, no I'll say shocked, and what all sells. After I was a few weeks into selling I started joking with my wife that literally anything will sell on eBay; there's someone somewhere in the world that wants what you have. After years of selling and making money I still believe this to be 100% true. Don't let numbers like 100 or more scare you – I promise you that you have 100, 120, and most likely tons more things just laying around that you can sell for around 10 to 15 bucks.

The final step in backwards planning to reach your goal is to determine how many listings you'll need to make the number of sales you arrived at. Not everything you list is going to sell within the first month or even longer. Most will, if you've done your research properly and price them competitively. To account for the ones that don't though we're going to factor in something the eBay community refers to as "Sell through rate" which is simply the percentage of your listings that end up selling. There are lots of different ways to really geek out over this stat to use it as a measure of your selling success, but for our purposes here, it's just going to be a simple percentage that we work into our equation.

From my years of listing and selling items, some that literally sell within hours of me putting them up and others that take months to sell, I'd estimate that 75% of items will sell within 60 days of being listed, again provided they're priced competitively based on historical research. So your last step is to divide the number of sales you got in the previous step, we'll use 120 to go on the high side, by .75 to give you the final count of items you need to position yourself to make $1,000. At a $10 average sale price (conservative estimate) and 75% sell through rate, you'll need to start out with 157 items to have enough firepower to make your first thousand dollars. Remember what we talked about a few paragraphs ago – don't let beginner's fear convince you that $1,000 isn't attainable. I'm pretty certain we all have 157 things or more that we don't need and can potentially sell for at least $10.

It's a natural next step to distill this down one level further and figure out how many items you need to sell each day to keep this pace, but I don't advise people to do that. Why? Because eBay is like the stock market. Ups and downs, hot and cold streaks, but in the long run if you're doing the right basic things, you'll end up to the good. I've gone days without selling something and I've sold half a dozen things in a matter of hours. While you can influence some of it as we'll briefly touch on in the next section, there's too much randomness involved to hold a hard daily sales goal when you're just starting out. I used to mentally look at my daily sales to know if I hit my mark, but if I didn't sell the average amount I'd need to each day I learned not to get worried because as long as I was being consistent with my work there'd be bigger days to make up for it.

So on that note, congratulations again! You now have your actual map that will take you to $1,000 in profit. You know what you have that you're able to part with because cash would serve you better, you know what on average each of those things sell for, and you know how many of the things you have available you'll need to sell to reach your goal. Consider this to mean your car is packed and gassed up for your ride to $1,000. In the final section we're going to turn the key and get moving so you can start getting paid along the way!

People Can't Buy What They Can't See – Now that you have your roadmap complete you want to think of your journey to $1,000 the same way that you think of a long road trip – by finding the quickest way to get there. Listing items is the gas pedal in this analogy; the more you list, the more you're going to sell. Even though there's some research that goes into being successful, a large portion of eBay is just a numbers game. Even if you do no planning up front (which I don't recommend, if you need any further convincing see the years it took me to get to where I'm at versus probably being able to do it in about five or six months had I known how to plan) you'll probably still make sales if you just keep listing things. Volume won't erase poor research and planning, but it can offset it. That's not how we're going to think though. Since you're already way more "eBay smart" than most people, your ability to quickly and regularly list items is going to be the kicker in getting you to your goal as fast as possible.

To list your first item, literally just get on your computer and do it. That's it. Go back to the section where we talk over each of the listing fields and start typing and clicking. After you've done that, do it again for another item. Honestly, listing your first 10 to 20 items should be nothing more than brute force on your part. Follow the instructions and get to work. When you're starting out you need to get a base of listings going because eBay definitely operates on the principle that active is better, so you want your account to continue pumping out new listings at a fast clip. When I was early on I'd aim for 5 new items a day, and most days I'd do more than that.

For your first 20 or so listings I recommend making an even split between auctions and Buy it Now listings. This will give you a chance to get comfortable with both and start to see the "eBay dynamics" that go along with each. For example, a lot of auctions won't get any bids for the first 5 days or possibly even until they're within 24 hours of ending. This isn't cause for alarm if you're selling pretty regular items, like the things that you cleaned out of your closet. Just see the process through and trust me, bids will come.

There are several eBay bidders out there that wait until the end of an auction to enter one bid and win the thing even though they can schedule their bids, so in a lot of cases you'll get a bid and a sale within minutes of each other right when you think your listing is just going to expire. Some Buy it Now items will get watchers but then mysteriously not sell while others will barely have double digit page views but sell within a day. Splitting up your listings is the only good way to learn all of this by seeing it at play. Just remember that on average, unless you have a pretty rare item (refer back to your selling price research to see how many listings for an item sold) auctions are going to bring in lower prices than Buy it Now items do, so factor this into determining which items you should list with each method. If an item already has a lower average selling price don't list it as an auction because there won't be much competition for it, thus driving an even lower price. Little things like this will start to sink in really quickly as you sell more and more.

Over time you'll start to come up with your own efficiencies that will help you get things listed much quicker. Think of listing items as the top of a funnel. In order for money (sales) to keep coming out of the narrow part at the bottom you have to keep heaping listings into the top so the cycle goes on and on.

The best way I've found to do this is to look at your life and schedule and figure out when you have pockets of available time. If you know that you can list an item in 3 minutes (this might seem way faster than you're able to go at first but after a few dozen your speed will improve dramatically) and you need to get five items listed each day then you need a block of at least 20 to 30 minutes (to account for stopping in between items, proofreading your listings – yes, you should do this, and other additional time.) This might be in the morning before you go to work, at night after your kids are in bed, even on your lunch break if you're grinding out a 9 to 5. Everyone's time is different, so figure out when you have it available and make a commitment to list each and every day. You're not going to always get things listed each day; even now I don't list each and every day, but you need to be listing on most days and try to never go more than a day without listing. As you get up and running you can be more liberal in your listing schedule, but when starting out it's pretty simple – people can't buy it if you don't have it up for sale, so you gotta list!

If you've done everything here as we've discussed it, from researching selling prices for the items you have to properly entering all listing information and writing an engaging and helpful description to taking quality photos, you should start seeing some sales come in within the first few days of getting started. When you do, make sure that you adhere to your shipping policy that you stated in your listing and that we talked about earlier. Follow the guidelines about which shipping service to choose and how to package and label your items that we went over previously. Get it in the mailbox or scheduled for pickup on time. Are you starting to notice a theme here? I hope so! Do what this book says and you'll be set up for success to the point that your learning curve will be much more accelerated than others.

Final Thoughts

Your eBay business is all mapped out, set up, and ready to go! Congratulations – seriously, take a moment to pat yourself on the back for all that you've accomplished, especially if you're a beginner and started from scratch.

Pretty awesome feeling, right? Of course it is.

The BIGGEST thing to remember about eBay by far is that it's not at all complicated to make a few hundred dollars of extra cash each month by just following the basic principles outlined in this book and being consistent with them. Don't overthink it and don't get yourself stressed and worried. Have fun with it!

I hope that you found this book useful and "worth the price of admission" in getting up and running on eBay. If you did, I'd greatly appreciate if you left a review wherever you purchased it. It doesn't take long, but leaving a review is a huge help not only to authors like me but also to other potential readers who are trying to decide if they'd enjoy and benefit from reading a particular book.

So stop what you're doing and please take a moment to go review this book now, before you get sidetracked with something else, because we all know how that goes!

Thank you again for reading and GOOD LUCK with your eBay journey!

www.ingramcontent.com/pod-product-compliance
Lightning Source LLC
Chambersburg PA
CBHW071803170526
45167CB00003B/1154